PRAISE FOR *CREATING YOUR RETIREMENT VAULT*

In 2010, I felt very strongly that the material I shared in my book Invasion Of The Money Snatchers *was timely and critical for those in and those approaching retirement.*

Since then the game has changed...ALOT. Justin Struble's book Creating Your Retirement Vault *addresses the economic changes that are relevant and with us today. So, regardless of whether you're already retired or preparing for retirement in the near future, the information Justin has gathered for you is timely, accurate and extremely important. Read this book!*

MATT ZAGULA

Author of Invasion of the Money Snatchers: A Practical Guide to Protecting Your Stuff from Creditors, Predators and a Government Gone Wild!

Justin Struble has written an amazingly informative and timely book on how to protect your financial assets and position yourself for carefree living during your Golden Years.

Every Baby Boomer should read and study what he has written.

STEVE CLARK

Sales & Marketing Coach

Owner of New School Selling

Justin's ability to take complex financial advice and put it in common sense terms is one of his unique abilities. He understands the real role of government in your financial future allowing you to be independent in your retirement. The FIXER is able to tailor make your retirement plan if you have 10, 20 or 40 years till you want to spend the rest of your life relaxing and doing what You want to do. If you have a fear of inflation, like I do, Justin can play it safe and still beat inflation. If You have a 401K, it may not be making the retirement money it can. Justin can show you ways that can make you more money.

Read, Learn, and Trust Justin.

KIPP GREGGORY
GM/Host WOSM
SuperTalk MS Gulf Coast 103.1

Creating Your Retirement Vault *is packed with great advice on how to retire optimally. It is simple and easy to understand. Many people believe that the success of one's retirement is about their ASSETS. That's not true! And Justin explains the importance of INCOME and RISK MANAGEMENT to the ultimate success of your retirement.*

TOM HEGNA CLU, ChFC, CASL
Best Selling Author of *Paychecks and Playchecks*

This book is full of practical, proven strategies to help you make it, keep it, and make sure it lasts indefinitely.

BRIAN TRACY
Entrepreneur, Speaker
Author of *The Psychology of Achievement*

Creating Your

RETIREMENT VAULT

Creating Your

RETIREMENT VAULT

Strategies to
Protect Your Investments
& Provide Predictable
Lifetime Income

JUSTIN STRUBLE

Advantage®

Published by Advantage, Charleston, South Carolina.
Member of Advantage Media Group.

ADVANTAGE is a registered trademark and the Advantage colophon is a trademark of Advantage Media Group, Inc.

Printed in the United States of America.

ISBN: 978-1-59932-500-2
LCCN: 2014946984

Cover design by George Stevens.

This publication is designed to provide accurate and authoritative information in regard to the subject matter covered. It is sold with the understanding that the publisher is not engaged in rendering legal, accounting, or other professional services. If legal advice or other expert assistance is required, the services of a competent professional person should be sought.

 Advantage Media Group is proud to be a part of the Tree Neutral® program. Tree Neutral offsets the number of trees consumed in the production and printing of this book by taking proactive steps such as planting trees in direct proportion to the number of trees used to print books. To learn more about Tree Neutral, please visit www.treeneutral.com. To learn more about Advantage's commitment to being a responsible steward of the environment, please visit www.advantagefamily.com/green

Advantage Media Group is a publisher of business, self-improvement, and professional development books and online learning. We help entrepreneurs, business leaders, and professionals share their Stories, Passion, and Knowledge to help others Learn & Grow. Do you have a manuscript or book idea that you would like us to consider for publishing? Please visit advantagefamily.com or call 1.866.775.1696.

DISCLAIMER

I, **Justin Struble, owner of Wealth CAPS**, created this book. If you would like to meet with me and see how/if I can help you implement safe money strategies, please go to my website www.WealthCAPS.com, where you can contact me directly. This book is intended to inform you and help you find ways to create your retirement vault.

Investment Advisory Services offered through Global Financial Private Capital, LLC, an SEC Registered Investment Advisor. Any comments regarding guaranteed income streams refer only to fixed insurance products. They do not refer, in any way, to securities or investment advisory products. Fixed Insurance and Annuity product guarantees are subject to the claims-paying ability of the issuing company and are not offered by Global Financial Private Capital.

Information is not intended to provide specific legal or tax advice. You are encouraged to consent your tax or legal professional for guidance on your individual situation.

The information and opinions contained herein are not intended as investment advice or an investment recommendation. It is solely the opinion of Justin Struble at the time of writing. It is given for informational purposes only and is not a solicitation to buy or sell the products mentioned. Past performance is no indication of future performance. Liquid securities can fall in value. The information is not intended to be used as the sole basis for financial decisions, nor should it be construed as advice designed to meet the particular needs of an individual's situation.

Author's Note

I got into the financial planning business to help people reach their financial goals. I live financial planning and breathe it. I always liked numbers and took a deep interest in investing and personal finance even as a kid. It wasn't until six years after I graduated college and decided to leave engineering that I got into the financial planning business. Very quickly I realized how broken the system was as I tried to find my role as a true advisor. I knew that over 80% of new advisors do not last more than three or four years. I think part of the problem is the focus on sales and major lack of focus on adding value and helping the clients. The two go hand in hand when the first priority is helping people. Sales come closely behind, but many of the large companies simply emphasize sales with little regard to the "helping clients" side. This will—and does—push good people out of the industry quickly.

Ultimately, I went independent within my first year in the business, and by the beginning of 2012 I had started my own company, Wealth CAPS. Since the beginning, I have always held the client's interests ahead of my own. I believe that trust is the foundation of each relationship and I feel that is the only way to run any business. When you meet with me, or anyone, at Wealth CAPS, you will stay in control. We are here to help navigate, but you are steering the ship. It is your financial plan; we are simply the coach on the sidelines giving you our best advice to help you succeed.

You will see as you read this book that I have made my niche in the retiree market. I want to protect your assets, help you earn predictable returns, and do so in an efficient and effective way for you to live a comfortable and independent retirement. This is the critical distinction between Wealth CAPS advisors and the advisors who consider themselves experts at high-risk/high-return investments. Or worse, the ones who think they are the best at everything. There should be a philosophy shift in your investments as you approach retirement, especially when you need retirement income from your investments.

I offer a no-cost, no-obligation consultation if you are interested in seeing if or how I can help you maximize your pursuit of happiness.

Rise Above The Mediocra-Sea!

Thank you,

JUSTIN STRUBLE
Financial Strategist
Wealth CAPS
(228) 334-5018
Justin@WealthCAPS.com

I'M NOT A BROKER ... I'M A FIXER!

Table of Contents

Introduction

There are certain core beliefs that I have and live by which guide me through my life.

AMERICA IS THE GREATEST COUNTRY

America rose to the top of the world through the free market capitalism that is our heritage: not from the presence of government, but the absence of government. The free market allows an individual to always make choices in his or her best interest, rather than in the best interest of the group as a whole. This is true even in a socialist society, but the lack of freedom makes cause and effect less apparent in a socialist society. In a free society, individuals must hold a higher moral standard, since their business and income are completely reliant on other individuals *choosing* to do business with them or hire them. This makes each sale or transaction inherently a win–win for both parties, since each side of the transaction has a mutual interest in benefiting from the transaction and providing the goods or services agreed upon to aid in all future transactions. When this is understood and accepted, you realize that the accumulation of wealth is simply a reflection of value that the person or company has provided over time.

WEALTH IS CREATED

You have the freedom to buy and sell whatever you want. You will buy something only if you want that thing more than the money you give up to buy it. The same is true for sellers. They will sell something, only if they want the money more than the product or service they provide. Thus, both sides of the transaction are better off when it is made, and the net result is an expanding economy (more wealth). Not only have the wealthy created their own wealth, but they have also similarly benefited everyone around them. As a business expands into new products or services, it spins off needs all around it, which can be filled by anyone interested in creating value in these areas. This is how the economy can continuously expand and people can be employed in new industries. The work force is constantly shifting into more-profitable fields and away from slowing or dying industries. This flow of labor, effort, and money is a critical element to future improvements in this economy and the world. America, a country of sellers and buyers, went from rags to riches in 200 years on this free-market concept.

"You can get everything in life you want if you will just help enough other people get what they want."

—ZIG ZIGLAR

LIMITED GOVERNMENT

The government should be in place only to enforce the fundamental laws of man—to punish people for fraud, theft, and violence. It is not the government's role to protect people ahead of time or to ever protect people from themselves. All other rights and wrongs should be left up to individuals. Let them set their standards and do business with those they trust and want to do business with. When the government tries to make life "fair," it ultimately enslaves everyone a little bit at a time.

These beliefs are a few of my guiding principles, not only in my own life, but also in my business, where I help my clients create their retirement vaults. This book is intended to help retirees or near-retirees create the retirement lifestyle they want— one with clarity of purpose and realistic expectations of what you can actually expect.

Do you demand a realistic, conservative financial plan for your golden years?

Do you want to create a plan that can provide you with the income and liquidity that you need throughout retirement?

You are in the right place!

You have gotten where you are, for better or worse, by the choices you have made over the years. This book will give you the foundation and resources to plan for retirement your way. When you meet with a financial planner you will be armed with this book as a resource guide on a variety of financial subjects. This book is intended to provide content-rich information in every chapter. The most critical years for your retirement investments are the five years before retirement and the first five years of your retirement. I lay out investments, strategies, and ideas for you to be able to make more-informed choices to help make those 10 years successful.

In today's economy, you must think differently. Investment theories that served in the past will not hold up going forward. You must question your assumptions and keep an open mind. I have successfully helped retirees design and live the comfortable retirement they had hoped for. The most important thing is to take action. Reading this book is a good start, but it doesn't mean anything if you do not take any action to improve your situation.

THE WORLD IS FLAT!

The world looks flat until you take a closer look. The financial world looks the same. There is an advisor on every corner in America and they all look the same until you look closer and start picking apart the pieces of their practice. Then you will start to see that all advisors are not created equal.

The financial industry as a whole has done a poor job of providing financial independence and security to clients, which should be their primary goal. You, the public, want and need to rely on the advice and service that you receive. Unfortunately, this is not the industry standard. Advisors are not held to a mandatory fiduciary standard stating that the advisor should put the client's best interest ahead of their own.

Traditional brokerage houses make money every time you switch investments with your advisor. The typical advisor works for the clients, but is often limited on the investment options they offer if they work for a large company. These companies have high sales quotas that the advisor must meet. This encourages advisors to make sales that may not be the best option for the client, not to mention that they may not even have a competitive option at that company, but still must sell it. Then there are the banks and accountants who have entered the financial industry acting as advisors. Since people tend to trust their bankers and accountants, the sales are made easily. The problem is that the decision to go into the financial service industry is often driven by the money that will be made from their existing customers. Even if the actual advisors at the bank are genuinely interested in helping the customers, they are still limited by the bank's available investments and products offered. This simply puts them on par with the captive, large company advisor.

Insurance agents have similar dilemmas and limitations. The problem is, many insurance agents are captive agents, and can only offer their company's insurance or annuity products. Some can offer a few different options, but it is only the independent agents who have the most options available to serve the client.

I believe the solution is in the independent advisors and insurance agents, which is why I went independent during my first year in the industry. This same shift is occurring all over the country. The large companies used to have a huge market share, but over the past several decades the shift from captive to independent has been remarkable. I see the best advisors and agents shifting to independence. As an independent agent, I am not tied to certain preferred products or pressured to meet quotas. As an independent, I hold myself to a fiduciary standard; this ensures that I am always working with the client's best interest in mind.

Most advisors are interested in helping you. Not all have the best solutions or investments for you, and not all of them hold your best interests above their own. You must determine which advisors are looking out for your best interest first, and who has the best available solutions. Then you can proceed with your financial planning process to build, fill, and secure your retirement vault to live the retirement you've always dreamt of.

This purpose of this book is to help you make your money do as much for you as possible to meet your goals. The first step is to identify your goals and concerns, which I will help you with in

Chapter 1. In Chapter 2, I will discuss retirement budget(s) and income sources in greater detail.

In Chapter 3, I will focus on the importance of avoiding losses from market volatility. This is probably the most important chapter of this entire book. In chapter 4, I will lay out an arsenal of safe investments and strategies. In Chapter 5, you will read about the "efficient frontier" and reducing your investment cost to improve your end results. In Chapter 6, I will lay out several strategies for magnifying your benefits (double-duty dollars) from those investment dollars that have been earmarked for a specific purpose. In chapter 7 I lay out several criteria that will help you determine who the right advisor is for you. How to evaluate the advisor and find someone you can trust to help you with your finances. Finally, I have included a bonus chapter that, while not directly pertinent to the main theme and conversation in this book, ties in with the subject and will likely be beneficial to some readers.

Chapter One

PURPOSE OF ASSETS

What is your money for?
Why did you earn it and what do you want it to provide for you?

I am going to address a few extremely important concepts and numerous smaller points through the next several chapters. The first step in proper retirement planning is identifying what you want your money to do for you. Without a clear purpose or endgame, you will try to make your money do everything. And, ultimately, you will see under-performance or missed opportunities. Only if you clearly define what you want your money to do can you properly evaluate risk/return and time/liquidity criteria to match your needs.

Let's look at what you might want some of your money to be used for.

- Income Now
- Future Income
- Real Estate Purchase
- Car/RV Purchase
- Future Medical Costs

- Inflation Hedge
- Long-Term Care
- Travel/Vacations
- Kids/Grandkids
- Charity/Philanthropy
- Other/Unknown Needs

For many of these items, you may not have a precise figure in mind. Setting up a budget for your retirement can help more than you realize. You have been methodical in your efforts to accumulate your wealth. Do not stop short on taking these final steps to keep your money working efficiently for you through your retirement.

If there isn't enough money to cover all of your needs or concerns, then you will need to prioritize. You may, for example, need to reduce your income to provide enough money for your other needs. Or it may be the opposite case. Some people keep too much money in liquid categories when they really should put it toward income or inflation concerns. Going through this evaluation process is only the beginning. As you read through this book, you will find there are several strategies that a good financial planner can help you with that may stretch your dollars further or even get them working double duty.

An investment has three discrete characteristics:

GROWTH   **SAFETY**   **LIQUIDITY**

You can **pick any two** of these for any given vehicle, but not all three. You may be familiar with the balance between risk and return. The higher the return you expect, the higher the risk of that investment. There is also a time trade-off with either growth or safety. If you need safety, then you will need to prioritize growth versus liquidity. If you need safety and liquidity, then you cannot invest in high-growth investments. Likewise, if you want safety and growth, then you cannot expect much liquidity with that vehicle. Later, I will discuss several choices to help you in this process.

Purpose of Financial Planning

Determining a more efficient and effective
strategy to reach your goals.

When identifying your purposes for assets and earmarking money for retirement income: You want to use as little of your money as possible to provide the income you need. This will free up the remaining assets to provide for the other needs you have in retirement.

Chapter Two

RETIREMENT INCOME

Cash May Be King, But Cash Flow Is Queen.

—JUSTIN STRUBLE

*The Most Important Financial Concept Retirees Need
to Understand Is Reverse Dollar Cost Averaging.*

—JOSH MELLBERG

When you retire, your mindset must shift. You must look at your assets and investments differently once you retire. You are not saving and contributing to your retirement accounts like you were while you were working. You may have heard the term "Dollar-Cost Averaging." It is the concept that you are contributing to your investments every month, and—despite the market ups and downs—you continue to invest monthly. This works as a stabilizer on your account. Now that you are retiring, you don't have this stabilizer. You may never put another dollar into your investments again. You are probably doing just the opposite. You are engaged in Reverse Dollar-Cost Averaging, which makes your account balance more volatile than it would be if you didn't touch it.

The other mental shift you must make is in the risk and volatility of your investments. Time is no longer on your side: you will be using your money sooner rather than later. If you will begin to withdraw income in the next five years, then you must plan around this. I am not suggesting that you settle for CDs or other returns that are less than inflation. I am suggesting that you avoid or eliminate losses on any money that you will use for future income by moving it to a more conservative vehicle.

As you enter or prepare to enter into retirement, you need to start planning your budget for the lifestyle you think you will live in retirement. This can often be a difficult process. To help with this transition into retirement, I recommend that you create three budgets: survival budget, standard expenses budget, and desired budget. These three budgets will help as you start to see what kind of income you will actually have in retirement.

The first budget is a **survival budget**—only the basics. It should cover all of the necessities: food, utilities, mortgage, taxes, medical, cars, etc. This will become your baseline. (I have an addendum in the back of the book that you can utilize to help with each of these budgets.) When you start your income planning, you must secure your income to provide everything on this survival budget.

The second budget you should create is a **standard expenses budget**. This should include everything in your survival budget, **plus** the next level of comfort. This may include extra money for eating out, hobbies, and vacation expenses. This standard budget would also include charitable giving and gifts for kids/grandkids, and other things you would like to do. This budget usually looks very similar to the lifestyle that you lived while you were working.

The last budget you should put together is the **desired budget**. This will include everything in the first two budgets, **plus** anything else you want to add. Tom Hegna, in his book *Pay Checks and Play Checks,* calls this the "Play Check budget." The standard budget would be the "pay check budget." This desired budget will have additional hobbies, maybe nicer cars, home improvements, and anything else you think you would like to do in your golden years.

Everyone is different, so you may need or want only one or two budgets. After you have your budget(s), it is important to think about how important it is to provide for each of these budgets. This will vary from person to person, and be dependent on how much income you will be able to produce in retirement. Some people will want to have the desired budget secured and coming in no matter what happens, while others may have their basic lifestyle covered and secure, but are willing to risk the stopping of "extras" if the investments run out. Knowing these things will help you as you look at investments for income, growth, emergency, or any other purpose.

SOCIAL SECURITY

Now that you are looking at retirement, it is time to put some real numbers to your social security benefits. There are hundreds of different ways to take social security. If you need the income at 62, then take it, but if you don't need it or if you are still working, then you will be able to receive more each year that you wait up to age 70. The complexity often comes in when you and your spouse can take social security at different times and even take spousal benefits and delay your own benefit until later. The social security website, www.ssa.gov, is pretty user-friendly and you can view your estimated social security benefit on the website. Software that can be used to optimize your total lifetime social security benefits is available, and your financial adviser should help you maximize these benefits by deciding when and how you collect social security payments. Social security is reliable and you can count on it continuing for the foreseeable future. It is safe to budget this income toward your basic living expenses without much concern for it ending.

PENSION

Pensions are not as common as they were a generation ago. If you do have a pension, consider yourself lucky. Pensions are not as reliable as social security, and depending on the company or government entity, it could be reduced or eliminated all together. If you know differently, you can rely on your pension to pay out for your retirement. In some cases, there is an option to take a cash payout, which would allow you to invest the cash and produce your own income, giving you more confidence in the income it will produce.

The payout you choose is important. You have to consider what will happen to your spouse's income if you pass away and what portion of your pension you want to leave for their income. Options vary from one pension plan to the next, so you will have to run the numbers on different scenarios to find best way to optimize your pension for your and your spouse's lifetime.

WITHDRAWALS FROM YOUR ASSETS

Once you have an idea of your budget and what income you will receive from Social Security and any pension, and when all of them will start, you can begin to fill in the remaining income gaps from your retirement savings. As you will see in the remainder of this book, it is important to separate the money that will be used for current and future income. This is important so you can invest this money for that specific purpose, and ultimately improve your financial plan as you work through it.

The biggest question retirees face in income planning is longevity risk. Americans are living longer. Even though you may not see yourself living to be 100, do not underestimate the possibility. You do not want a retirement plan that allows you to outlive your income.

A 65-year-old couple has a 50% chance that one of them will live to 92 years and a 25% chance that one will live to 97 years.

If you determine that you do not have enough retirement income, then a reverse mortgage may be an additional source of income or cash to help you provide the lifestyle you need through retirement. This is a discussion with many variables. I am not implying that this is something everyone should do or consider, but it is a legitimate tool at your disposal. If you are short on income and need a little extra, discuss the potential of a reverse mortgage with your financial planner to see if it makes sense for you and how you can best use a reverse mortgage.

ANNUITIES FOR INCOME

Annuities have been around for a long time, but they have been changing significantly over the past decade. Historically, annuities were bought like a pension. You would literally give your money to the insurance company and they would provide a lifetime income for you, or for you and your spouse. The insurance company took the risk of longevity away from you. Now we call this type of annuity an immediate annuity, and the trade-off of your money for a lifetime income as annuitization. In today's low-interest-rate environment, these immediate annuities, and annuitizing, do not make sense for retirees looking for income from their money. Most people can get a higher income from one of the annuities that I am about to mention; additionally, they give up control of the money when it is annuitized. Hence, if you and your spouse pass away in two years, then the insurance company keeps the chunk of money—not your heirs. There are many different variations of these immediate annuities. I want to discuss the advances in some other types of annuities and their ability to provide retirement income.

The next big advancement, which happened in the 1980s and 1990s, was the popularity of variable annuities. Variable annuities allow you to invest in the market with your money, but you can purchase riders (guarantees) that give you a lifetime income and/or a death-benefit protection on your money. As you can imagine, in the '80s and '90s when the stock market was skyrocketing, the variable annuities were great for market upside and some protection on your money if the market dipped at the wrong time. The primary drawback with a variable annuity is the high cost that you pay each year. They regularly cost 3–5% per year. This can really eat into your growth when the market is not skyrocketing.

Since 2000, the indexed and hybrid annuity markets have developed significantly, and at just the right time. After the market crashes of 2000 and 2008, they have become extremely popular, for many reasons. Typically, their costs are much lower than a variable annuity. Their best feature is that they participate in market gains, but do not participate in losses when the market goes down. If you own an indexed annuity or a hybrid annuity, you won't have to worry about losing money when there is a crash. On the flipside, you will not earn as much if the market skyrockets. But this should be of less concern for retirees, as I will discuss in further detail in the next chapter. You have worked a long time and have retirement within your reach. The piece of mind you have with these annuities, knowing you cannot lose money, outweighs making large returns and exposing yourself to the risk.

Another primary benefit of a hybrid annuity is the higher income available. The insurance company does not need to worry about your account disappearing with a large market crash, so they are able to pay you a larger percentage of your money each year on a guaranteed basis. This enables the issuing insurance company to increase the percentage that you can withdraw over a similar variable annuity. A hybrid annuity offers other features valuable to retirees, such as a bonus and healthcare multiplier, which will be discussed later.

These hybrid annuities continue to evolve. Currently, only a handful of hybrids with an alternative index exist. These alternative indexes control the market volatility. This gives the investor more consistent returns, which is a critical part of providing retirement income. The two important benefits for this type of retirement income discussion are the high retirement income for life and the avoidance of market losses while still participating in the gains. Over the next several years I expect dozens of hybrid annuities with these alternative indexes will appear—which will give you, the investor, even more options.

Chapter Three

AVOIDING LOSSES

Avoiding stock market losses is paramount in securing your retirement income. Market losses will destroy your ability to withdraw a predictable retirement income.

WARREN BUFFETT'S RULES OF MONEY

Rule #1:

Don't Lose Money

Rule #2:

Never Forget Rule #1

AVOIDING LOSSES

Avoiding stock market losses during retirement is the most important aspect of your retirement income plan. You have to change your thinking as you approach retirement and start withdrawing an income from your investments. I am going to show you how losses in your retirement account are more damaging than it will be to simply earn a lower return using a more predictable investment.

You have been told, "The greater the risk, the better the return." This is usually the case, and you can see this relationship in the *efficient frontier* graph (Chapter 5). It shows the trade-off between risk and return (when investing efficiently). The logic has been that investing in higher-risk investments produces higher average returns and this is correct, but there is more to it than that. If you have decades to sit and wait while your investment grows, then the average return is the most important factor in how your money grows. If you are currently withdrawing an income or you plan to start drawing an income in the next five years, then you need to look a little harder at the investments you use and the returns they will produce year to year. You must focus on avoiding losses more than on averaging high returns. The important thing to remember is: "The Sequence of Returns" matters more than the "Average Return." Let me explain this point, because most people (and even most investment advisors) do not fully understand it. I didn't until I saw the numbers and ran them for myself. To show you exactly what I mean by the importance of the sequence of returns, let me give you an example with three scenarios— keeping the average return the same over 10 years, but changing the sequence around. This example is simplified, but it produces realistic results.

AVERAGE RETURN VS. REAL RETURN

First, let's assume that the stock market averages 10% returns. We all know it doesn't earn exactly 10% every year. To make it more reflective of actual stock market volatility, we will assume that every even year it earns 30%, and the odd years it loses 10% [30% + (-10%) = 20% / 2 = 10%]. This gives us a good estimate of the actual stock market volatility (measured as a standard deviation).

The first lesson to learn is the difference between *average return* and *real returns*. The average return is simply adding 30 x 5 and -10 x 5 [so, 150 + (-50) = 100] and dividing by 10 years, to get an average return of 10%. This is simply the *average of the number*. The real return is a little more difficult to calculate. To calculate the *real return*, you have to multiply the returns by each other and not simply add them together. You must remember to add the original principal when calculating your return which will be represented by 1. For the 30% (0.3) return we earn we will multiply 1.3 and for -10% returns we will multiply by .9 [1 + (-.1)]. Since we are multiplying these returns together to come up with the real return percentage, we will need to take the root of the total. In the following tables we will look at a 10-year period and therefore the real returns will be based on the 10th root. The simple math will get you close, but as you will see in this chapter, it can be significant, especially if you are withdrawing money from your investments.

Year 1	30.00%		130.00%
Year 2	-10.00%		117.00%
Year 3	30.00%		152.10%
Year 4	-10.00%		136.89%
Year 5	30.00%		177.96%
Year 6	-10.00%		160.16%
Year 7	30.00%		208.21%
Year 8	-10.00%		187.39%
Year 9	30.00%		243.61%
Year 10	-10.00%		219.24%
			219%
Average Return	10.00%	Real Return	8.17%

Bad Timing:

5% Withdrawl	>	10% Average Return

A bad sequence of returns can turn an otherwise good decade (10% returns) into a negative environment for your investments.

This compounding of returns is the first reason you don't want losses in your investments. The more consistent the returns, the higher the real return becomes.

SEQUENCE OF RETURNS

Now that you have seen how the volatility of returns can affect your real return, it is time to address the most important consideration, which is the *sequence of returns* while you are withdrawing income from your retirement savings. ***This is the most important concept in the book.*** To illustrate, we are going to use the same returns I laid out earlier (30%, -10%, etc.) over a 10-year period. I will examine three different sequences: average, best, and worst. These sequences will not affect money that is not being withdrawn for income. In each of these three scenarios, we will look at a 10-year period and we will keep the same 10 returns we showed earlier; we will simply rearrange the order and you will see how much your *real return* is affected by the *sequence of returns*. We will assume the initial investment is $100,000 and you are withdrawing $5,000 (5%) per year from your investment.

Scenario #1: Average Sequence

In our first scenario, we have $100,000 and a withdrawal of $5,000 (5%) per year over a 10-year period, with an *average return sequence* alternating each year between +30% and -10% return.

	Returns		Balance	After Earnings	After Withd	
Year 1	30%		$100,000	$130,000	$125,000	
Year 2	-10%		$125,000	$112,500	$107,500	
Year 3	30%		$107,500	$139,750	$134,750	
Year 4	-10%		$134,750	$121,275	$116,275	
Year 5	30%		$116,275	$151,158	$146,158	
Year 6	-10%		$146,158	$131,542	$126,542	
Year 7	30%		$126,542	$164,504	$159,504	
Year 8	-10%		$159,504	$143,554	$138,554	
Year 9	30%		$138,554	$180,120	$175,120	
Year 10	-10%		$175,120	$157,608	$152,608	
Average:	10.00%	Ending Balance =	$152,608			
				Net Return:	Withdrawl:	Return:
			$152,608	4.32%	5%	9.32%

As you can see from this chart, the real return in this scenario was 9.32% (4.32% after withdrawals). We were able to withdraw 5% each year and still grow our account balance from $100,000 to $152,608—which is good. This is the same return scenario from the previous chart. So, how are the return percentages different? Because the bad return happened to a lesser number because of the 5% withdrawals ($112,500 instead of $125,000).

Scenario #2: Best Sequence

We have seen what an average sequence will do for us, now let's look at the *best possible sequence of returns*. In this scenario, we will assume that we earn 30% returns for the first five years, and then lose 10% for the second five years. This will frontload our best returns, while still averaging 10% returns over the entire 10 years.

	Returns		Balance	After Earnings	After Withd.	
Year 1	30%		$100,000	$130,000	$125,000	
Year 2	30%		$125,000	$162,500	$157,500	
Year 3	30%		$157,500	$204,750	$199,750	
Year 4	30%		$199,750	$259,675	$254,675	
Year 5	30%		$254,675	$331,078	$326,078	
Year 6	-10%		$326,078	$293,470	$288,470	
Year 7	-10%		$288,470	$259,623	$254,623	
Year 8	-10%		$254,623	$229,160	$224,160	
Year 9	-10%		$224,160	$201,744	$196,744	
Year 10	-10%		$196,744	$177,070	$172,070	
Average:	10.00%	Ending Balance =	$172,070			
				Net Return:	Withdrawl:	Return:
			$0	5.57%	5%	10.57%

When we frontload the best returns, you can see that our *real return* is even higher than the average, and in this scenario our real return was 10.57% (5.57% after withdrawals). Just like in the average return scenario, we were able to withdraw 5% each year and still grow our investment balance. In this case, our balance grew from $100,000 to $172,070 over these 10 years (almost $10K more than with the *average sequence* of returns).

Scenario #3: Worst Sequence

Now that you have seen the best, let's look at the worst sequence. As you would expect, the worst sequence comes when the negative 10% returns come in the first five years and then the 30% returns come in the second five years.

	Returns		Balance	After Earnings	After Withd.	
Year 1	-10%		$100,000	$90,000	$85,000	
Year 2	-10%		$85,000	$76,500	$71,500	
Year 3	-10%		$71,500	$64,350	$59,350	
Year 4	-10%		$59,350	$53,415	$48,415	
Year 5	-10%		$48,415	$43,574	$38,574	
Year 6	30%		$38,574	$50,146	$45,146	
Year 7	30%		$45,146	$58,689	$53,689	
Year 8	30%		$53,689	$69,796	$64,796	
Year 9	30%		$64,796	$84,235	$79,235	
Year 10	30%		$79,235	$103,005	$98,005	
Average:	10.00%	Ending Balance =	$98,005			
				Net Return:	Withdrawl:	Return:
			$98,005	-0.20%	5%	4.80%

In this *worst sequence scenario*, you can see that your real return is significantly reduced, down to 4.80% (-0.20% after withdrawals). This means that our investment balance has gone down from $100,000 to $98,005 (after we removed 5% each year). Notice that the difference between the worst and the average is significantly more than the difference between the best and the average. This gets to the crux of the issue. **Losses affect your investment more than gains do.** This is one of the reasons that avoiding losses during retirement is so critical to your financial success.

IMPORTANT NOTE: 10% is less than 5%. The "10%" average return is less than the 5% withdrawal, since the balance has gone down after 10 years.

COST OF INVESTING

Now that you see how your real return is affected not only by volatility, but also by the sequence of returns, let's look at one more factor. How does cost come into the real return? When the market earns 10%, you may not be able to earn that full return with your investments. There are several ways to reduce your costs, but we are not going to go into them in this chapter. For now, let's assume that the cost of ownership/management over your investments is 2%. This will be a reduction of *both* your average and real return on your investment. Look at the three charts below that reflect the three scenarios we just looked at when discussing the sequence of returns. Notice that I am reducing the 30% returns down to 28% and the -10% returns down to -12%, to show the returns you will see on your investment. Recognize that paying an extra 2% for the same quality of investment can drastically drag down the real return that you see on your investment.

Average Return Sequence With 2% Cost:					
Initial Investment: $100,000			Withdraw $5,000 per year		
	Returns		Balance	After Earnings	After Withd.
Year 1	28%		$100,000	$128,000	$123,000
Year 2	-12%		$123,000	$108,240	$103,240
Year 3	28%		$103,240	$132,147	$127,147
Year 4	-12%		$127,147	$111,890	$106,890
Year 5	28%		$106,890	$136,819	$131,819
Year 6	-12%		$131,819	$116,000	$111,000
Year 7	28%		$111,000	$142,080	$137,080
Year 8	-12%		$137,080	$120,631	$115,631
Year 9	28%		$115,631	$148,007	$143,007
Year 10	-12%		$143,007	$125,847	$120,847
Average:	8.00%	Ending Balance =	$120,847		
				Net Return:	Withdrawl:	Return:
			$120,847	1.91%	5%	6.91%

Best Return Sequence With 2% Cost:					
Initial Investment: $100,000			Withdraw $5,000 per year		
	Returns		Balance	After Earnings	After Withd.
Year 1	28%		$100,000	$128,000	$123,000
Year 2	28%		$123,000	$157,440	$152,440
Year 3	28%		$152,440	$195,123	$190,123
Year 4	28%		$190,123	$243,358	$238,358
Year 5	28%		$238,358	$305,098	$300,098
Year 6	-12%		$300,098	$264,086	$259,086
Year 7	-12%		$259,086	$227,996	$222,996
Year 8	-12%		$222,996	$196,236	$191,236
Year 9	-12%		$191,236	$168,288	$163,288
Year 10	-12%		$163,288	$143,693	$138,693
Average:	8.00%	Ending Balance =	$138,693		
				Net Return:	Withdrawl:	Return:
			$138,693	3.33%	5%	8.33%

Worst Return Sequence With 2% Cost:						
Initial Investment: $100,000			Withdraw $5,000 per year			
	Returns		Balance	After Earnings	After Withd.	
Year 1	-12%		$100,000	$88,000	$83,000	
Year 2	-12%		$83,000	$73,040	$68,040	
Year 3	-12%		$68,040	$59,875	$54,875	
Year 4	-12%		$54,875	$48,290	$43,290	
Year 5	-12%		$43,290	$38,095	$33,095	
Year 6	28%		$33,095	$42,362	$37,362	
Year 7	28%		$37,362	$47,823	$42,823	
Year 8	28%		$42,823	$54,814	$49,814	
Year 9	28%		$49,814	$63,762	$58,762	
Year 10	28%		$58,762	$75,215	$70,215	
Average:	8.00%	Ending Balance =	$70,215			
				Net Return:	Withdrawl:	Return:
			$70,215	-3.47%	5%	1.53%

Simply by reducing your returns by 2%, you can see that with the average sequence your real return was reduced 2.41% from 9.32% to 6.91% (1.91% after withdrawals), and the balance after 10 years is $120,847 instead of $152,608.

On the best sequence with 2% cost, the real return was reduced 2.24% from 10.57% to 8.33% (3.33% after withdrawals). The best sequence is less affected by the cost of ownership and management since the cost represents a smaller portion of the return. The balance after 10 years is $138,693, much less than the $170,070.

With the worst sequence and 2% cost, the real return was reduced 3.27% from 4.80% to 1.53% (-3.47% after withdrawals). Notice how simply adding a 2% cost reduced your real return by 3.27%. **This is why cost is such a big concern, especially when you withdraw an income or when the market performs poorly.**

The balance after 10 years becomes $70,215, which should make you very concerned about how long you will be able to live on your investments going forward.

TAKEAWAYS

Even though the *average return* is 10%, the *real return* that you actually realize is much less. Consequently, you should be very passionate about completely eliminating losses from your retirement investments as you approach and are in retirement.

This one issue is why I say the most critical years for your retirement lifestyle are the five years before you retire and the first five years of your retirement. A large loss during those 10 years will set you back for years to come.

ADDITIONAL THOUGHTS

Here are a few other items for you to think about.

First, in my examples, I kept the 10-year average return at 10%. What if the next 10 years average 0%? How ugly will the real return be for your investment (30,408; -6.22% real return)?

Second, what if you need more than 5% of your money each year? If that's the case, the effect that the sequence of returns has on the real return on your investment balance will be exaggerated. That is why most advisors recommend you withdraw only 3–4% each year, to avoid the risk of running out of money. What they are really doing is reducing the effects of a bad sequence of returns. In reality, you don't have to settle for such a low withdrawal rate. You just cannot make investments that expose you to large losses. In

---

Any comments regarding safe and secure investments, and guaranteed income streams refer only to fixed insurance products. They do not refer, in any way to securities or investment advisory products. Fixed Insurance and Annuity product guarantees are subject to the claims-paying ability of the issuing company and are not offered by Global Financial Private Capital.

this book I will show you ways to withdraw 5–7% safely without the concern of running out of money. (So you won't run out of money before you run out of life.)

Third, historically, advisors have used a *bucket strategy* to mitigate this sequence of returns risk. Unfortunately, the traditional buckets (CDs, US Treasury bonds) are not very good options in this low-interest-rate environment. Typically, there is a 1-5-year bucket, 6-10-year bucket, and a 10+-year bucket. What happens if over the first 10 years you use up the first two buckets as expected, and the 10+ bucket has not grown due to flat market returns? Not to mention inflation over those 10 years. Now you will be forced to reduce your withdrawal rate or risk running out of money. Not a good retirement strategy. This is the problem retirees face today in our new economic environment.

SUMMARY

The issue of avoiding loss in your investments is always an important concern, but when you start drawing an income from your investments, it becomes arguably the most important factor in your retirement plan. This does not mean you should settle for CDs or fixed accounts that avoid losses but don't even keep up with inflation. That is not a satisfactory solution, either. This chapter was designed to stress how both the importance of avoiding losses as well as the sequence of returns are to your success in retirement. Now we can focus on these concerns throughout the remainder of this book and help you create your retirement vault.

Chapter Four

SAFE INVESTMENTS IN TODAY'S ECONOMY

The perception of what a safe investment is has changed over time. Frankly, it varies from person to person. The market, real estate, and the economic crash of 2008 reminded people just how risk averse (loss averse) they really are. Historically, the common philosophy was simply to shift from stocks to bonds over time, and that would protect you as you approach retirement. They used to say an acceptable withdrawal percentage was 5–6% per year. Now, with the same strategy, they are recommending 3–4% to avoid running out of money. This is a flaw in investment strategy, not in the withdrawal rate during retirement. Unfortunately, when the market crashed in 2008, even bonds were hit hard, which is one of many reasons why the old investment strategy does not work today.

The highest priority for most investors is the absolute safety of their investment dollars. People are still wary of the stock market, even though it has recovered from its 2008 losses (although real estate and jobs are still depressed). This is not an irrational demand for safety; indeed, it is a rational response.

Here's why:

- First, your investment account is not tangible like real estate, so when it loses value you don't really know where it went or what will bring it back.

- Second, as you get closer to retirement and you build up your nest egg, you begin to focus on preservation instead of growth. This is important, since you will not be able to rebuild your wealth after you retire and stop saving.

- Third, your investment account has been built by hard work and diligence over time, and it is difficult to see it diminish, even by small amounts.

These are the primary reasons why most people, especially retirees, demand safety of value first, and only after it is secured do they focus on earning a higher return. This is why so many people have shifted to CDs (Certificates of Deposits) and money market accounts from stocks and bonds. Shifting to CDs has protected their money from losses, but now that interest rates are at record lows, they don't earn much of anything on those CDs. CDs have always been a part of retirement strategies (and, in some cases, a significant part, using CD Laddering), but the current super-low interest rates have made that a failing strategy. More importantly, some economists predict these low interest rates may be the status quo for several years and even up to a decade. Let me be clear: CDs do what they say they will do, but they are not a good investment for a long-term purpose in today's economy.

We have established that if safety is the primary concern (as it should be for many people), then traditional bond and stock market investments are too risky to rely on. CDs are not much of an improvement. They are better in the short term, but not in the long term. This dilemma is even more frustrating in 401(k) plans. Many 401(k) plans do not have a truly safe option for your nest egg; this is true for some Fortune 500 company plans, and most small company plans. You are left to try and time the market, which you cannot do, or to shift to cash or a money market account as you approach retirement, leaving some growth potential on the table.

BE CAUTIOUS OF THE HYPE

Before I elaborate on types of safe investments, let me address a few strategies that claim to be safe but need to be vetted before you put your hard-earned money in them. First, let's look at **High-Yield Bond Funds**. Many advisors label these high-yield bonds as safe investments; what they really mean is that they are less risky than other options. Remember, when you are listening to an advisor who only deals with the market, "safe" really means "relatively safe." If you are in a bond fund, you are also diversified across multiple companies, limiting your risk to an individual company defaulting. However, high-yield bonds are not safe enough for the standards we are going to establish here, because they can still lose value. They are called high-yield bonds for a reason, and it is because the company borrowing the money has a higher risk of default (not paying). The bonds receive interest payments regularly. They are also less affected by changes in interest rates, which is why it is common for advisors to recommend them. If interest rates go up, then the price of bonds goes down, but the price of high-yield bonds will be hurt less than will low-interest rate bonds. As a bond mutual fund, they are required to keep most of your money invested in the market (in this case, high-yield bonds), so even if the market looks bad for all high-yield bonds, they will continue to invest in them as long as you own the fund. This is the problem with most mutual funds; they cannot get out and sit on the sideline when the market is crashing. All in all, high-yield bond funds can be a part of a portfolio, but they can lose value as well and should not be used as majority.

The second investment many advisors define as safe, but which might not be safe enough, is **Dividend Stocks**. Typically, these are large, established companies that have a long track record of paying a dividend. Since you, the owner, will receive dividends regularly as an income stream, these are generally safe companies to invest with. You can buy individual stocks, mutual funds, or Exchange Traded Funds (ETFs) to invest in dividend stocks. ETF's are index funds which are designed to track the market or a portion of the market instead of attempting to beat the market like Mutual Funds try to do. Since these are typically stable companies, the value is more stable, and the dividend is usually fairly low. Unfortunately, the price of the stock can and will go up and down over time. This means that, even though they pay the dividend consistently, you (the owner) may actually lose money if the stock price drops. The other risk is that the company stops or reduces the dividend. This can produce a cascading effect if you and the other owners (investors) sell off the stock, further eroding its value. This happened to the extreme in 2008 with banking companies that many advisors considered safe investments, and even companies like GE. Everyone saw prices crash and, consequently, reduced dividends.

I am not suggesting this will happen again or that dividend stocks are bad. On the contrary, they are good investments, but they may not meet your standard of low risk. Just remember:

dividend stocks can lose money, and will, from time to time. Do you see how an advisor's definition of safe and your definition of safe may differ?

Real Estate is the third investment whose safety I want to address. Real estate is easy to like since you can see it and "use it." First, let's separate the investment from the work or job of investing in real estate. Many real estate investors claim that real estate makes better returns than stocks. The part they overlook is the work involved in putting profitable real estate investments together. There is a huge difference between buying stocks or securities and buying a property down the street, when you factor in closing costs, repairs, management of the property, maintenance, etc. Yes, you can make huge profits from real estate, but these profits are based on your skills and work (a job) involved with finding and acting. The underlying real estate is simply another investment.

When we look at real estate as an investment, we can see that it can be bought in various ways on the securities market (REITs, Master Partnerships, Land Companies, etc.). These investments all act and produce returns similar to other types of investments. Some pay high dividends, while others are more speculative investments. I offer some of my clients a real estate option using a Delaware Statutory Trust (DST). The clients can sell their real estate and 1031 exchange the money into the DST, allowing the client to avoid current taxes that would have occurred otherwise. This is great for tax savings, and my clients can typically earn decent returns without dealing with the day-to-day "work" involved with the investments. The drawback is that this is not a liquid investment. So, you can't call up next week or even year and get your money. You get the income from it, but not your principal. This investment, like most non-stock market real estate investments, is limited by your liquidity, and, most importantly, you can lose money. Either of these limitations makes real estate investing a risky endeavor.

RETIREMENT VAULT TOOLS

I want to break up retirement vault tools into two categories. The first category is "stable" investments. Some are better than others in certain situations. You do need to keep some of your money in these *stable vehicles* for your emergency funds or for short-term cash needs. These types of investments should be used only as PART of your retirement vault.

The second category of retirement vault tools is designed, first, to not lose money and, second, to outpace inflation. I will call this category *strategic vehicles*. Each has pros and cons, and **they should not be your first choice for short-term cash or your emergency fund**. Over time, some of them can become your short-term cash reserve, but that is not their primary purpose.

Stable Vehicles

The first "stable" vehicle is your **Money Market** account. Money market accounts are very common. They are offered through banks and investment companies. They are currently paying out next to nothing in interest. They are effectively savings accounts. There is no penalty for withdrawing money from them, or any age restriction or limit for using them. When they are FDIC insured, they are fully protected from losses. When investment companies offer money market mutual funds, they are only backed by the company offering them. But even in 2008, they kept their value. In some cases, the government stepped in and backed these companies. This may not happen again. But when you put your money in a money market account at an FDIC-insured bank, it is safe. The obvious flaw is the lack of interest. If we assume that inflation is 3% and your money market earns ½%, then you are safely losing 2½% each year.

The second "stable" savings vehicle is the infamous **Certificate of Deposit** (CD). CDs have set time periods, usually between six months and five years, and there is a penalty for early withdrawal, which is usually three-month's interest. But you will not go below the amount of your initial investment. CDs are FDIC insured, which protects your account from losing money. You do not have to be 59½ to withdraw a CD, since there are no tax benefits with a CD. The money is liquid even considering the penalty, since it is small and cannot cause you to lose any of your initial investment. Unfortunately, the interest rates are around 1% currently. This makes your CDs just like the money market account. They will lose 2% (3% inflation minus 1% interest) each year. I like to call them a safe place to lose money.

The third "stable" savings vehicle is a **Fixed Annuity**. Annuities are actually insurance products. I like to call fixed annuities glorified CDs. Just like a CD, they have a time period, typically three to seven years. The interest is usually around ½–1% higher interest than a CD with a similar term length. The drawback of fixed annuities is that they are less liquid. You can usually withdraw a portion without any penalty each year (typically 10%). Beyond that, you will incur surrender charges, causing you to lose some of your principal investment. This is the only way that you can lose money, since the interest is set for the term of the annuity. If you may need your money before the term is up, then this is not a "stable" vehicle for you. The other caveat is your age. Fixed

CREATING YOUR RETIREMENT VAULT

annuities, like all annuities, are tax-deferred structures, which is an added benefit. Unfortunately, this also means you cannot take money out until you are 59½ without a penalty. This makes them ineffective for anyone who might need the money before reaching 59½. But if you will be at least 59½ when the term is up, then a fixed annuity may be a better option than a CD. A fixed annuity will still under-perform inflation, so it is not a long-term play.

The fourth "stable" vehicle is **Short-Term Bond Funds**. I want to broaden this vehicle to include funds that are focused on preservation and income, as well. This doesn't include most conservative investments, but would include a fund that does not go down for more than a few months; the return is typically below inflation, but still higher than bank CDs. As you can tell, this vehicle is difficult to define, but let's outline its characteristics in a bit more detail, and hopefully that will help to clarify the criteria.

Short-term bond funds are liquid and available to buy and sell without any penalty. There would be no age restrictions or tax advantages. There is a chance that you could invest and lose money in the very short term (< 3months), but it would not take long to recover, due to the nature of short-term bond funds and income/preservation driven funds. If you see a fund that you think may fit this mold, but it earned significantly more than inflation in one year, then you don't have the right fund. That is too great a return for what is realistic for this type of vehicle. That is part of the reason it still makes the cut as a "stable" savings vehicle. Such a fund would be a good place to keep your short-term cash, and the small amount of risk is probably tolerable, given the upside of earning over a several-year time period more than you would with money market accounts, CDs, and fixed annuities. But if a guarantee of no loss is critical, then this is not for you.

The fifth and final "stable" savings vehicle is a **Single-Premium Life Insurance** policy. Single-premium life insurance used for this purpose is less well-known, but it is extremely effective. One limitation is that you must be insurable in order to invest in this vehicle. That is why you may hear this called a "preferred savings vehicle," since not everyone is eligible. Many types of single-premium life insurance policies exist, so let me be clear which ones would make the cut as "stable" savings vehicles; that is, those policies that have 100% principal protection from day one. This means that you cannot lose money even if you change your mind a week later. They insure that you can get your full investment back. Your age is important with these policies. Because this is a tax-deferred vehicle intended for retirement, the government will penalize you if you withdraw money before you reach the age of 59½. How your money earns interest varies by insurance company. Part of your earnings will pay for the cost of insurance, since you are using a life insurance policy as your "stable" savings vehicle. Obviously, you will have a death benefit attached to this policy that will be greater than the investment you put into the policy. The exact amount depends on the insurance company and your age and health. Many of the new policies also provide a Long-Term-Care rider, which is an additional way to access your money on a tax-free basis. Usually this doesn't cost any more, but some companies may charge for it. Even after these costs of insurance are paid for from your earnings, you should still see a reasonable return each year. The return is tax deferred, and is only taxed if you withdraw money from policy. The return is not guaranteed, but your principal is always guaranteed. Unfortunately, most people brush this vehicle off simply because they say they don't need life insurance—but if it beats a CD on the earnings, is

CREATING YOUR RETIREMENT VAULT

more liquid, and you qualify, and you get a death benefit if you don't need to use this money—then why wouldn't you want your money to work double duty instead of sitting in a CD working single duty? Don't overlook this "stable" savings vehicle.

Strategic Vehicles

"Strategic vehicles" are designed not to lose money and to outpace inflation. In order to outpace inflation, you will have to give up some of the "stable" attributes, but that is the necessary trade-off to keep from losing real value long term. We have already discussed why you need to keep some of your money in the "stable" vehicles, but since they don't keep up with inflation, you need to put most of your safe money in one or more of these four "strategic vehicles."

The first strategic vehicle is a **Conservative Market Allocation**. Many of you have heard of asset allocation, which is a strategy to invest your money over several asset classes to diversify, in an attempt to smooth the ride of the market roller coaster. Asset allocation is a very important aspect of diversifying your investments. Equally important is the conservative concentration of your investments. This will lower expected returns, but will give you much less volatility. Even if the market has several losing years in a row, with a conservative allocation you may see only one negative year, and even that loss will be much smaller.

This strategic vehicle does not come with any guarantees, but it will also allow you additional earnings when the market has good years. A conservative market allocation is a good halfway-point between fully investing in the market and putting everything in CDs. You can find a conservative market allocation as a mutual fund or an Exchange Traded Funds (ETF). I am a firm believer in ETFs and the cost savings you will gain with them over mutual funds.

The second "strategic vehicle" is called **Conservative Managed Money**. In the past, managed money investing used to only be available to multimillion-dollar accounts, but not anymore. Most managed money accounts can be opened with $25,000–$100,000, depending on the company. The value of a managed money account is the active management of your investment. The management team is able to trade when an opportunity arises, but more importantly, they can shift a significant amount to cash when nothing looks like a good investment. This alone allows them to smooth the volatility of the market. The cost is also reduced over mutual funds, giving you, the investor, more of the earned returns. Additionally, to secure your money in both good and bad times, it is important to invest in a conservative portfolio run by a conservative money manager. I work with a company that has done extremely well at preserving principal first and foremost, and only then looking to produce income and growth. They have been able to maintain this high standard while avoiding losses, with their constant pursuit of value and stability in their investments. However, even with conservative managed money, there are no guarantees. You can lose money. It is critically important to invest through a money manager and team whom you have confidence in.

The third "strategic vehicle" is **Cash-Value Life Insurance** (CVLI). CVLI is often given a bad name by people who either don't understand how it works and what it actually does, or by people citing situations where it has been used inappropriately. This "strategic vehicle" is built inside of life insurance, so, yes, you must be insurable. This vehicle works best for someone who has at least 10 working years before retirement, as well as a death-benefit beneficiary if you were to pass away prematurely. CVLI is a permanent life insurance policy that is over-funded to the maximum non-MEC level, which is something that should be discussed with and explained by your agent when you are setting it up. This strategy is most effective for monthly savings while you are still working and putting money away. The only reason this is not labeled a "stable vehicle" is that your cash value (money you can get out) will be less than you put in as premiums for the first 6–12 years. This does qualify as a "strategic vehicle," however, because you will be able to outpace inflation on a tax-free basis as long as you keep the policy in force. Typically, this money will not be used in the first 5–10 years, but long term it is an excellent savings vehicle. I use this vehicle to save for a future car purchase, a child's college fund, and even future retirement income. This is not for the undisciplined saver, or for money you may need in the first several years. But for long-term savings, it is tough to beat this "strategic savings" vehicle for someone still working. Most critics try to compare this to stock market returns, but it serves a different purpose. It is not meant to be high risk, high return. It is meant to be safe and predictable growth.

The fourth "strategic vehicle" is a **Hybrid Annuity**. Hybrid annuities are a creation of the last decade and are built out of an indexed annuity. As I mentioned earlier, all annuities are tax-deferred vehicles and, thus, are designed for money that will not be used until you are 59½ or older. Let me explain how an indexed annuity works. Insurance companies may charge fees for each benefit. The cost varies by company and will be disclosed to you when you sit down with an advisor and see a specific illustration. When you invest in an Indexed Annuity, you may get a bonus (typically 5–10% of your initial principal). Sometimes this incurs as an annual fee, but usually it will not. Your money and the bonus are linked to a market index (often the S&P 500), but your money has downside protections. If the index loses money over the year, then your money does not go down. On a good year, you participate in the gains. Depending on the issuing company, either your earnings will be capped, or the first portion of any gains will be taken as a fee. As an example, let's assume the index drops 10%; you would not lose any money. The next year, the index gains 10%; you may be capped and only earn the first 5%, or the company may take the spread (fee) and take the first 3%. In that case, you would make 7%. This is why I say that you participate in the gains. You will never earn the entire index, since they are insuring that you don't lose any money in the bad years. Once your money goes up, you lock that gain in and you cannot lose it the following year. This concept of avoiding losses and retaining gains is extremely valuable as you approach and/or are in retirement.

To make this a hybrid, we have a couple of additional benefits. First, you have an income value that will be at least equal to, but often greater than, the account value. This income value goes up each year and is used to determine how much income you can withdraw as a guaranteed lifetime income. The insurance company will pay you this income for life when you trigger it, and even if the index underperforms and your account runs out of money, they will continue to pay you the same income for as long as you live. The other feature that is part of a hybrid annuity is a healthcare multiplier. In general, a healthcare multiplier will double your income for a certain number of years (typically five) when you qualify for long-term care. Usually there is not a fee for this rider, but some companies may charge one. When you qualify, this multiplier is paid even if you stay at home and have a spouse, family member, or friend take care of you. After the doubler has ended, your income will go back to the original amount you were withdrawing. The hybrid annuity is not a "stable" investment vehicle, because there are limitations on how much you can withdraw for several years. Typically, you can only withdraw 10% per year without incurring surrender charges. An index or hybrid annuity should not be used for money you need to withdraw in the next few years. The surrender charges can eat into your principal. However, these surrender charges are waved if you qualify for long-term care, are terminally ill, or die. The surrender charges are designed to keep people from switching companies every couple years.

Hybrid annuities were specifically designed for retirees who need current or future income. Companies offer different options, so it is important that you find the one that fits your needs the best. Some companies even offer a death benefit option for money from which you don't need income, but intend to leave to your heirs.

We have gone through five **stable vehicles** for your short-term money and emergency funds. These are the most predict-able, but are not designed to outpace inflation. Then we covered four **strategic vehicles** that will avoid losses, and still outpace inflations. It is important to limit the amount you keep in "stable" places and to shift the excess to "strategic vehicles" that, while still extremely predictable, will also grow your value long term. These are the tools that I use for my clients, my family, and myself to help build our vaults so we can enjoy retirement.

Because these decisions and issues are so important, when you decide to implement or incorporate these tools into your plan, I urge you to seek the advice of a financial professional. Choose someone you can trust to advise you: someone who knows your specific situation and who will keep your best interest in mind.

Chapter Five

COST VS. EFFICIENT INVESTING

"The miracle of compounding returns is overwhelmed by the tyranny of compounding costs."

—JOHN BOGLE

"I really think an index fund that just charges a few basis points for management is pretty hard to beat."

—WARREN BUFFETT

In this chapter, I hope to give you a better understanding of what you are paying for and what degree of risk or volatility you should expect. Obviously, the less you pay, the better off you are—as long as the investments are comparable. It should also be apparent that the lower the risk, or the less volatile the investment, the better. This should be the theme of your discussions with your financial planner. Not, "How much do you charge?" but rather, "How much do you charge and what reductions in risk are you giving me for that cost?" I know that is a mouthful, but follow me through this process so you can ask the right questions when the time comes.

EFFICIENT FRONTIER

You may have heard about the **efficient frontier** before, or perhaps your advisor showed you the graph and where your investments fall on the curve. The efficient frontier implies that the market is efficient. This is fairly accurate, although some people will argue that the stock market is more of a semi-efficient market. Either way, what does that mean for you? It means that a company (stock) that is expected to earn a certain return has a certain level of risk associated with it. So if you see two stocks that are expected to earn or grow the same amount, then they will have an equal amount of risk or loss, or, on the upside, of outperforming expectation. If this weren't the case, the price of the riskier investment would drop until the risk/return corrects to the proper point on the risk/return curve (efficient frontier). All things are not equal, and there are inefficiencies in the market in the short term, as things change and fears and emotions play a role. But for this discussion and for your investments, you should assume that the market is efficient. Here is the efficient frontier graph for our discussion:

As you can see, the higher the return, the higher the risk associated with that investment. There are several important things I need to point out that pertain to the efficient frontier.

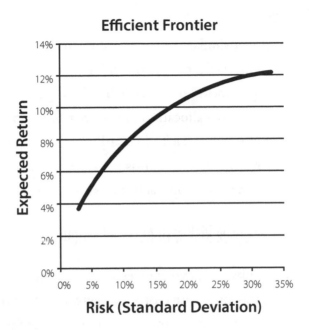

Diminishing Benefit

Note that the efficient frontier is not a straight diagonal line. As you increase the expected return, you take on significantly more risk (volatility) as you move toward the right end of the graph. The opposite is true on the left end of the efficient frontier. As you reduce risk, you get a diminished benefit. This diminished benefit leads most people toward the middle region.

Diversify

The efficient frontier is based on a single investment. When you buy or invest in 20 or 50 securities (stocks) that are at the same or very similar points along this graph, you are able to reduce your risk a little bit while still maintaining the same expected return. This basically means that the curve as a whole shifts to the left slightly when you look at a diversified investment.

Asset Allocation

Asset allocation is a similar concept to diversifying your investments, but it is a diversification across different asset classes (large cap stocks, foreign stocks, short-term bonds, high-yield bonds, etc.). When you use asset allocation in your portfolio, you gain an additional level of stability (lack of volatility). This works to shift the curve further to the left, and thus enhance your investments. The exception is when you approach the extremes of the curve.

·················· **Reduce Risk with Asset Allocation** ··················

It is difficult to truly spread your investments among asset classes when you are ultra-conservative or very aggressive. So instead of simply shifting the entire curve to the left, it only shifts the middle section of the curve, which gives the same final result of simply diversifying: the end points of the curve will be the same. This doesn't matter for most investors in the middle of the curve, but the conservative investor who may need income should recognize that asset allocation at that extreme of the curve is not really providing much benefit. Having all bonds will result in more volatility than an asset allocation with some stocks included. Other vehicles referenced in the previous chapter will fill this need better than simply investing in the market, and will be explored in the following chapter.

TIME

The longer you hold an investment, the more vertical this curve becomes. Put another way, the risk or volatility over time is much less than it is over the next year. In the short term, your investment will follow this curve very closely, but if you hold the investment for 5, 10, or 20 years, then the risk of loss becomes significantly less. In any given year, the risk is still there, but for you to go below your original investment balance becomes less and less likely each year. That being said, if you have time to invest, you should shift up the curve to benefit from a higher average return in the long run. How far you are willing to shift is based on your risk tolerance, time frame, and other factors.

So, if you are looking at a point on the curve that has an expected return of 10% and a level of risk (standard deviation) of 18%, then you have a decent chance of losing money in a given year, but over 20 years you should expect to have averaged between 7% and 13%. This means you will outperform another investment that is expected to earn only 4% over just about any 20-year period. Therefore, you should shift up the curve if you have time, or shift down the curve as your retirement needs come closer. That being said, I don't know many people who like or can tolerate 30–50% losses in a given year, so don't shift so far up the curve that you change your investing philosophy when the next bad year comes along. The worst thing you can do is to realize you were too aggressive only after you have lost half your money.

RISK AND STANDARD DEVIATION

"Risk" is a vague term that needs to be addressed and quantified. Thus far, I have been talking about risk in terms of standard deviation. It can also be quantified as alpha or beta. You can look at risk and the likelihood that you will lose some money—or even all of your money. To avoid this doomsday scenario of losing all of your money, you need to diversify and use an asset allocation to meet your goals. To quantify the percent chance you have of losing money or quantify how much you could lose in a given year, *standard deviation* is the best measure.

Standard deviation is a measure of how volatile the investment or portfolio is. The best way to describe the standard deviation is with a graph. Here is a theoretical bell curve showing the expected returns in the middle and the standard deviations on each side on a $1,000,000 portfolio invested in the S&P 500.

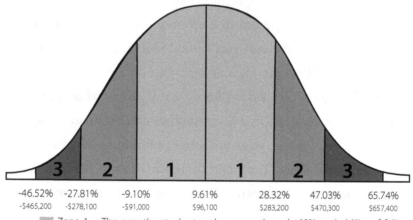

Portfolio Value:	$1,000,000
Average Return:	9.61%
Standard Deviation:	18.71%
Current Risk Tolerance:	Aggressive

3	2	1	1	2	3
-46.52%	-27.81%	-9.10%	9.61%	28.32%	47.03%	65.74%
-$465,200	-$278,100	-$91,000	$96,100	$283,200	$470,300	$657,400

Zone 1 = The assest's actual return has approximately 68% probablility of falling within this zone (i.e. within 1 standard deviation of the asset's expected return).

Zone 1 + 2 = The asset's actual return has approximately 95% probability of falling within this zone (i.e. within 2 standard deviations of the asset's expected return).

Zone 1 + 2 + 3 = The asset's actual return has approximately 99% probability of falling within this zone (i.e. within 3 standard deviations of the asset's expected return).

Within one standard deviation (zone 1), you will see 68% of the expected returns. That means in two out of three years, the return will be within that range. The rest of the time, the return will be more or less than that range. When you look at two standard deviations (zones 1 and 2) away from the average, 19 out of 20 (95%) annual returns will be within that range; likewise, in 1 in 20 (5%) years the return will be above or below this level.

Once you understand this relationship, it is very easy to see how likely a certain investment is to deviate from the expected return—and more importantly, how far below it could deviate. This is invaluable in making sure that your investments meet your risk tolerance and, more specifically, that your short-term investment risks are compatible with the purpose of that money.

COST TO INVEST

The investing world has been turned on its head over the past 20 years and looks to stay that way well into the future. Investing continues to get better for individual investors and families. The Internet has given everyone access to investment research tools (charts, comparisons, etc.), not to mention all of the online investment websites where you can trade your own account without ever dealing with an advisor. This alone has pushed down the price of trading. Competition and the free market is a beautiful thing. You can go to one of these websites and trade for less than $10 per trade, a fraction of what you would pay at a traditional location. I work with a company that allows my clients to regularly trade for as little as $1–$2 per trade.

Another huge breakthrough is the abundance of index funds, aka Exchange-Traded Funds (ETFs). ETFs allow you to get diversification and even assets allocation in as little as one investment. This means you can invest in one ETF, pay for only one trade, be invested along the efficient frontier, and not have to pay anything—even taxes—until you sell the ETF. The other benefit of an ETF is the low cost of management. ETFs drop the cost of management well under 1%, and often less than ½%. Compare that to the average mutual fund, which costs around 1.5%. This does not mean that mutual funds do not have a place for some investors, but when cost is a concern, ETFs are the solution. And, again, they are tax efficient and no taxable event occurs until you sell (unlike mutual funds).

John Bogle, the founder of Vanguard, wrote *Common Sense on Mutual Funds*, an insightful book about stocks, bonds, mutual funds, ETFs, and the relationship between them. If you buy his current tenth anniversary edition (which you should), look at the figures on pages 10, 17, and 416. These three figures will reiterate the points outlined in this chapter.

WHAT ARE YOU PAYING FOR?

In today's economy you can invest on your own, do your own research and trading, and still keep your cost below 1%/year. If you want to be your own advisor—and are competent to be so—I would recommend this course if you want the cheapest solution. It may not be the best or the least costly, but it will be the cheapest. It takes time and energy to become competent. But if you have money sitting there that you won't need for income (or any other purpose) for a while, then the level of competency required is fairly low for long-term investing. On the other hand, if you are trying to manage your own money and need it for income now or in the near future, or want to try and outperform the market, be prepared to spend a lot of time and energy becoming even more competent. Managing your money on your own creates constant, additional demands on your time and energy.

If this isn't for you, then what should you expect to pay an advisor—and what value should you receive from working with one? When you work with a professional, you are paying for several things: management of the investment, rebalancing or asset allocation, trading, financial planning, and the reduction or elimination of risk.

The first thing you pay for is the management of the investment. The person you meet with is not usually the person making the actual trades and decisions; it is typically done with the mutual fund managers your advisor invests with. The average mutual fund cost is approximately 1.5% per year. Some are better than others; if you pay attention, you can get this cost down to 1% or less.

Another activity you pay for is the rebalancing or asset allocation. This is typically done quarterly or annually when you meet with your advisor and readdress your goals, concerns, and the future outlook. Sometimes this is charged as a flat fee, and other times this is a percent of the investment balance (usually <1%/ year of your Assets Under Management). Some advisors do not charge anything extra for this service.

Depending on what company you invest through, you will also pay for the trade/investing transactions. This can be as high as $50/trade or as low as $1–$2/trade. This basic trading fee pays the necessary cost to the actual stock exchange for the transaction. The rest of the cost is paid to a middleman, your advisor, the advisors company, or some combination thereof.

When I invest for clients, not only do they pay the lowest trading cost in the industry, but I also use managed money portfolios, which keep the cost down. The investments are also constantly rebalanced inside of the portfolio.

The biggest benefit you can receive from meeting and working with an expert is financial planning advice. This is difficult to quantify and often overlooked, since you don't know what you don't know, and even the financial planner doesn't know what specific advice or insight will benefit a specific client. Financial planning services can cost anywhere from $200 to $15,000 per year. I firmly believe in the value of a financial plan. Too many so-called advisors end up as product peddlers. They get a person in front of them and find a product to push him or her into. A true financial planner does not talk about investments or products until he determines what a person's actual needs are. Only then will the advisor try to solve the problem. This process requires a little more work, but the client will get real advice, not simply the hot product of the month.

The other feature you will pay for is the reduction or elimination of risk. This is typically done by an insurance product, anything from a CD to an annuity or life insurance policy. There are hundreds of products, and each one works a little differently. You are guaranteed not to lose money, but you cannot move more than 10% of your money during a given year. This trade-off protects the insurance company: you cannot move your money after the company has just protected you from a decline in the market. Investing in any of these products will be comparable to the cost of investing in the stock market. The cost will vary drastically from product to product, but should not be out of line with any other investment. The biggest cost is the liquidity limitations of your money, which is the trade-off for getting the guarantee. For most people, this is not a cost, since they have no plans to move or use the money for years, anyway. Others see this as a cost, since they have plans for the money or have not thought that far ahead to know if they may need the money in the near future.

When you total the cost of investing, managing, and trading your money, as well as financial planning advice, you should demand that your cost is less than 2% per year. The more money you have, the lower this cost should be. As you approach $1,000,000 invested, you should see the total cost approach 1% per year. Unfortunately, too many people who get financial planning advice have not had good investment management or asset allocation/balancing, and are still paying 3–4% or more in cost. As you can imagine, this level of cost and mismanagement will drag your asset growth—if not stop it altogether.

You can determine the cost of a given investment on your own by going to www.PersonalFund.com. *Put in the ticker symbol and you will be shown the real cost. You will usually be given an alternative investment that is available at a much lower cost, but which still meets the same investment goals. I use this to help me put together cost analysis for my clients' portfolios.*

In summary, efficient investing requires not only the appropriate risk/return investments for you, but also proper financial planning and a low-cost solution for all your needs. Do not underestimate the importance of each aspect of proper financial advising. Assets allocation is critical to your investments' success and stability. Financial planning is important not only to get a better handle on your goals, but also to alert you to risks you may not be aware of. Even I, someone who loves financial planning and investing, would not have been as well informed on certain investments and strategies if I had not learned from other financial experts around me. Lastly, high costs can negate any growth potential you could have. It is beneficial to get your costs below 2%. The way you pay the advisor may not necessarily line up with what he or she is being paid for, and this can be confusing.

Chapter Six

DOUBLE-DUTY DOLLARS

Double-duty dollars: In which you put your money in one bucket and the money serves dual or even more purposes. When comparing double-duty dollars to regular investments, it is important to compare apples to apples, whenever possible. Planning ahead is the other critical component of utilizing double-duty dollar strategies. If you don't have a plan or don't know where your money is going or coming from, then it is difficult to actualize the real value of these double-duty dollars.

Before exemplifying double-duty dollars, I want to lay out what your money should do for you. First, you want your money to grow and work for you. Second, your money should protect you and provide for what-if scenarios. Third, you want to do this in a tax-efficient manner to maximize your money's effectiveness. Once you know this, it becomes a question of how much money you are spending today versus how much money is working for your tomorrow.

When we go through these examples of double-duty dollars, you will notice many of them are based on insurance products. This is done for two main reasons: (1) to protect or insure something, and (2) it often provides a tax-efficient structure for your other money.

EMERGENCY FUND EXAMPLES

You need an emergency fund whether you are still working or already retired. The rule of thumb is three to six months of living expenses. This amount will vary greatly from family to family, but everyone should have an emergency fund. One strategy is increasing your insurance deductibles to lower your premium for your home and auto insurances; when you have enough money in your emergency fund, you are still protected if you have a loss. This is a simple financial planning strategy to help your dollars work a little harder for you.

Most people leave their emergency fund money in a savings account or Certificate of Deposit (CD) at the bank. Unfortunately, this is a lazy use of your money, as it does not keep up with inflation while the money sits in the bank—not to mention that the money is taxed every year that it sits there. Here are two examples that will help your emergency fund work double duty.

Home Equity. If you have enough equity in your home, you can get a home equity line that will work as your emergency fund. This shouldn't cost you anything to set up and will allow you access to this money (equity) if or when you do need it. This allows you to put the money that was your emergency fund toward something that is working for you, and not just sitting in a bank.

Life Insurance. If you are over 59 ½ and are insurable, this may work well for you. There are life insurance policies that allow you to put money in once, and keep it 100% liquid. That means it can be taken out whenever you need it and you are guaranteed to get your money back, maybe even more than your original principal payment. That alone isn't special, but there are more benefits. While your money is in this bucket, the first benefit is the life insurance, which is some multiple of the amount you put in this bucket. The other big benefit is long-term-care insurance, which is also a multiple of the amount of money you put in this bucket. When you put your money in this type of policy, it becomes a triple-duty dollar strategy. You can use it for any of the three features or combinations of them. Depending on which insurance company you work with, you can also earn a solid return on your money that should outpace inflation. Additionally, while your money sits here, it is tax deferred and both the death and long-term-care benefits are completely tax free. So think about this: You put your emergency money in this bucket, hoping you don't need to use it, and while it is there you have effectively doubled your money (tax free). If something does happen to you, or you pass away or need long-term care, that doubled money is waiting for you.

BUNDLING EXAMPLES

These don't need as much explanation, but I will mention several of them so you don't overlook these simple double-duty dollar strategies.

Car and Home-Owners Insurance. You can often get a discount when your car and home-owners insurance are with the same company. This doesn't mean it is always better or cheaper, but it is something to consider.

Long-Term Care on Both Spouses. Typically, you can get a couple's discount when both spouses get long-term-care insurance from the same company. This is not always the best option, but something to consider.

Life Insurance with Long-Term-Care Insurance. Many of the newer life insurance policies have a free rider for long-term care. This allows you to use some or all of the death benefit toward any long-term-care needs that might arise. This is one of many reasons to review your old life insurance policies. This benefit is usually free, so you are truly getting something for nothing.

Life Insurance with Disability Rider. You have an option when you buy a life insurance policy of having a disability rider who will pay the life insurance premium for you if you become disabled. Since disability insurance policies don't replace 100% of your income, it is very helpful not to keep paying your life insurance premiums if you become disabled. It is a small price to pay to get a much-needed benefit. Not all of these riders are created equal, so the insurance company and your insurance agent are important factors.

SAVINGS EXAMPLES

Combining your savings with other benefits is a great way to utilize money you were already putting toward a future purchase and to gain additional benefits along the way.

Replace Permanent Life Insurance. Many old life insurance policies have a good level of cash value in them, but a bad outlook for their future, given the current interest rate environment. Even if you have plenty of cash value in your policy, it is important to get your policy reviewed—especially if it is older than 10 years. Life insurance policies have changed a lot in the past 10–20 years. If you are in good health, then it is very likely that you will be able to supercharge your cash value going forward by rolling it into a new life insurance policy. When you do this, you can change the death benefit and premiums you are paying and get all the new bells and whistles, while having a more efficient policy going forward. Your new policy should be working at least double duty compared to some of the old clunkers I have seen.

Perpetual Motion Machine. You read that correctly. I can create a savings vehicle that will pay for all of your future car purchases. While you are saving, you will also get life insurance with all the previously mentioned features of the newer life insurance policies (double-duty dollars at work once again). You do need to be insurable for this strategy. Your car payments can be locked in for life, even if you want more expensive cars each time you purchase another vehicle. You also get a death benefit that increases over time, as well as long-term-care benefits from the death benefit amount, which will go up as the death benefit and the cash value increases. The disability rider means that if you become disabled, not only is the life and long-term-care insurance paid for, but all of your future car purchases will also be paid for by the company. This turns out to be a quadruple-duty dollar strategy, and while you are saving in this perpetual motion machine, you should expect decent returns year after year, even in this low-interest-rate environment. This is a tax-free return when properly borrowed against the policy and the policy is kept in force.

RETIREMENT EXAMPLES:

Some of these structures have been around for a while and will be familiar to you. They still have double-duty benefits that can enhance your retirement plans when used correctly.

Roth IRA. The Roth IRA gives you both tax-free growth and tax-free use of your money. You can actually use your contributions at any time, and the earning can be used after 59 ½ as long as you have had the account open for five years or more. This flexibility gives you more options for the investments and still keeps the tax advantages of a retirement vehicle. This gives you double-duty dollars, as your money grows tax free, but you can withdraw the contribution without any penalty and use it for another purpose.

401(k). You get tax-deferred growth on your 401(k), but the real benefit is when your employer matches or automatically contributes to your 401(k) Plan. This is free money that turns this retirement vehicle into a double-duty dollar strategy.

Freedom-Building System. The freedom-building system is similar to the perpetual motion machine. The details of the system are different, but conceptually they work within the same process. You would be investing inside of a life insurance policy, which gets you the tax-free growth of a life insurance policy. You also get the long-term-care benefit and disability protection on your premium, which will continue to fund your life insurance, long-term-care insurance, and retirement fund if you become disabled. Depending on the strategy you use inside of the life insurance policy, you can earn decent returns year after year, and do it on a tax-advantaged basis. This is also a quadruple-duty dollar strategy.

Hybrid Annuity. Although other types of annuities can give you double-duty dollar strategies, the hybrid annuities offer the most valuable benefit to many retirees and near retirees.

First, you typically get a bonus on your money when you invest in a hybrid annuity. In some cases this bonus is in real dollars, and other times it is only a bonus to your income base, which is simply a calculation number and not real money. Make sure yours is a real bonus and not just an income-based bonus.

Second, your investment is indexed to the market, which means you participate in the market gains, but do not participate in market losses. This is exactly the philosophy that retirees drawing income need the most. As I laid out earlier, the losses while you are withdrawing an income will devastate your real return. This indexing strategy avoids the losses, and even though you don't get all of the market upside, you end up in a much safer position with a higher expected real return.

Third, there is typically an option for an income guarantee, so you can receive a lifetime income for you, or you and your spouse. This income rider guarantees that even if the income you receive draws down the balance to $0, the issuing insurance company will continue to pay the same income to you for as long as you or your spouse lives.

Fourth, if you choose the income option and then become confined to a nursing home or need home healthcare, then the income will increase (typically double) for a certain period (typically five years). If you are still alive after this healthcare multiplier runs out, the income will go back to your previous lifetime income level and continue for as long as you live.

This hybrid annuity is not only a quadruple-duty dollar, but it also fits the needs of so many retirees who are looking for the most income from their assets, without the risk of running out of money. The only restriction on these hybrid annuities is the liquidity. Generally, you can get no more than 10% out per year without a penalty. This should not be an issue if you are using the money for income, since you don't want to use it up prematurely, anyway.

As you can see, there are plenty of tools you can use to stretch your money a little further. I have laid out some of them here, but there are others. Most of these require you to plan ahead and be responsible with your money in order to maximize its benefits. When you do this, you are able to capitalize on long-term factors that maximize your long-term goals. Many of these double-duty dollars become more valuable when you are doing comprehensive planning. When you do this with a financial planner, gaps in your plan that you may not have seen with individual investment advisors or insurance agents become more visible. This is just one more reason to meet with a financial planner and develop a comprehensive plan. When you do, it will be much clearer where to utilize some of these double-duty dollar strategies in your financial plan.

Chapter Seven

CHOOSING THE RIGHT ADVISOR

Choosing the right advisor is important. Advisors may seem like a commodity; it seems like you can just pick anyone, and that all advisors give the same advice. This is not the case. The advice you receive can be very different depending on the experience, the company that pays them, and maybe even the products that pay a financial advisor. For better or worse, you will get different recommendations after meeting with several advisors. This means that you need to maintain control of your decisions and make sure that you understand what choices are being made when you do meet with an advisor. Here I have laid out five factors that need to be considered when choosing an advisor, along with several "feel-good" items that may help you decide between the final few.

COMPATIBLE PERSONALITY

This can be the most important criterion. If you have an advisor you do not trust, then you are not likely to follow his advice, even if it is correct. Conversely, if the advisor doesn't relate to or understand your concerns, then your advisor may be advising you on something that may not fit your actual goals. Either can be detrimental to your future advisor relationship, and, more importantly, to your assets and your ability to reach your goals. Communication and honesty are fundamentals in the relationship between you and your advisor. A good stream of communication can build a strong understanding and result in a successful strategy to reach your financial goals and address financial concerns.

Does the advisor spend an appropriate amount of time meeting with you? Do you feel that you are the number-one priority when you meet with him? If not, will they put the same level of effort and attention into your investments? Get answers for all of you questions and make sure you are confident in the advisor you choose.

TRANSACTIONAL VS. RELATIONSHIP BUSINESS

Most advisors do a decent job of building a long-term relationship with their clients, but there are exceptions. The insurance industry, for example, generally falls short. When I say insurance industry, I am specifically talking about the insurance that directly pertains to your finances (life, disability, long-term care, annuities). Traditionally, these have been sold as transactional products, where the agent sells the policy and has little or no follow-up year after year to insure that the policy is still right for you. As consumers, you probably view this as a one-and-done transaction, since that is how they have been done so much in the past. But as your life circumstances change, so should your protection elements.

In some cases, you, the client, only want a transaction. You may go to an insurance agent and say, "Here's the insurance policy I want. How much is it going to cost me?"—but there may be a better way to get what you want and need that you may not be aware of. You should have a plan when you talk with your agent, but I encourage you to go in with an open mind to see what other options the advisor may have to offer.

Bottom line: Look for an advisor who can competently advise you on *all* aspects of your finances and match your actions to your goals and concerns. Piecemeal advice from several advisors on different items is not the way to go. You want a comprehensive financial planning process that looks at the big picture and lays out a strategy for reaching your goals in the most efficient way possible. When you meet with this type of advisor, your advisor should be making every effort to get to know you and understand your desires. If you don't feel this is the case when you first meet, then they're not the right advisor for you.

BUSINESS SUPPORT AND RESEARCH DEPARTMENT

Your advisor has some external support, and this becomes more critical for you if you have a sizable amount of wealth. If you are just starting to save, then this is less critical to you. It is more important to address the other factors mentioned here. For the rest of you, it is more important to know what support your advisor is receiving—and from whom. An advisor who works for a large company may be getting a lot of support and information, but it is typically top-down advice and may not be as unbiased as you would want. If an advisor is independent, but only sells insurance, then he is receiving information from insurance companies on products, laws, concerns, etc. However, this may be selective information and skewed. A well-balanced advisor will be receiving information from the market side (stocks, bonds, etc.), from the insurance side (annuities, life, disability, long-term care), and from independent sources. Having several sources of information allows the advisor to filter the information and determine what information is skewed or biased and what information is important.

From the consumer's side of the table, it is difficult to tell what information the advisor receives and bases his expectations on. One way to find out is to ask the advisor what types of business he does and what types of business he does the most of. If the advisor says he can do investments and life insurance, and then you find out that most of the advisor's clients are investing only in life insurance, then you may want to reevaluate how open the advisor is to other investment vehicles. This doesn't mean that two people with similar situations shouldn't be using the same strategy and tools, but it does mean that if all of their clients are using the same strategy, then the advisor probably isn't well balanced. A good advisor will have a specialty in an area which he is an expert, but not just one product. This is good; it means that the advisor has excelled and can bring that expertise to help you. Just make sure that's not the only thing he does, that he's not a one-trick pony.

HOW ARE THEY PAID?

Advisors can get paid three ways. None is inherently better or worse than any other, despite what some people may say. The advisor may get paid in all three ways, but not in multiple ways from the same advice or investment.

The first way, which I mentioned previously, is with a fee. Fee-only advice is when you pay the advisor either by the hour or for a specific financial analysis. This is typically done annually, but with wealthier clients it can be done quarterly or even monthly if the client and advisor agree to its importance. The fee that is charged can vary greatly. It can range from $200 to $20,000, depending on many variables. Usually, it is based on your total assets. Some advisors have set amounts for certain portfolio analysis levels.

The second way advisors can be paid is based on the insurance products they write. This means when you buy life insurance or an annuity, the advisor gets some percentage of the premium. When this occurs, the amount the advisor gets does not come out of your investment. It is simply included in the product, along with all the other administrative costs that the insurance company must pay to be in business. The amount the agent receives can vary greatly and it is not consistent among a specific product line. Some policies will pay the advisor half, or all, of the first year's premium, while others pay a small percentage every year. Annuities typically pay a percentage of the investment, much like a real estate commission when you buy a house. Thankfully, this means you don't really need to worry about what they get paid; you just need to make sure that the option they present to you is the best for you—and not the best for them.

The third way an advisor gets paid is by assets under management. This means they are investing for you, and have your investments in either mutual funds or managed money accounts. This pays the advisor some percentage of the assets you have invested. Usually, this pay to the advisor is between ¼–1% of the assets invested. Don't get confused—this is not the total cost of investing. There is also a management fee. With mutual funds, there are several other fees and costs, which are disclosed and hidden. But as far as the advisor's pay, it generally will be somewhere in that range. This means if you invest $1,000,000 and the advisor earns ½%, then he is paid $5,000 per year to advise you.

An advisor can get paid by any and all of these three sources; having multiple sources of income will allow him to earn his way without pushing one option exclusively and focusing on transactional business to make a living. An advisor cannot get paid from multiple sources on the same advice.

CERTIFICATIONS AND LICENSES

Your advisor must hold certifications and licenses. In order to do business, they must be licensed in each area that they work. To sell life insurance, they must be licensed. To manage investments, they must be licensed. To buy and sell stocks, they must have another license. To get paid for financial advice (fee-based), they must be licensed as well. Then there are continuing education requirements for each state and for most lines of business that the advisor uses.

Above these basic licenses and education requirements, many advisors will get additional certifications. The most well known is the CFP, Certified Financial Planner, but there are many others that let you know the advisor has taken additional certifications to specialize in a specific field. A word of caution: having certifications can be deceiving. They may have taken additional courses and advanced their careers, but it doesn't really mean much when it comes down to your specific situation. Someone could be a so-called expert but not bring any more value than the guy next door who doesn't have the certification. You can ask them about their certifications and get an understanding of their training, but just like everything else, you have to evaluate for yourself what and who is going to serve you best.

FIRM SIZE/RESOURCES

An advisor working for a large company (one most people have heard of) does give you the confidence that they have resources behind them that will help support you. In the past, the larger firms would provide valuable training as well. Over the past generation, however, the level of agent training has steadily declined. Now the big firms are focused on the immediate payoff. They look for sales at all cost and do not really care if the advisor lasts a year, let alone makes it a career. This leads to low-quality advice and a cold-call mentality. The senior advisors may be better at these firms, since they may have been brought up correctly, but many of them have a similar mentality.

So what are your other options? Independent agents are where you will find your best value. Independents have more flexibility. This can lead either to excellence or to mediocrity. An independent agent does not have quotas to hit, which takes some of the pressure of selling off the advisor. But it may lead to the advisor doing just enough to scrape by. The advantage of independence is the advisor's ability to structure his practice as he sees best. Nowadays, there are so many resources for independents to build off of that they are often better equipped to help you than are the large companies. Resources and software exist for the independent advisor that would have been cost prohibitive a few decades ago. Now the independent can compete with—and outperform—the large firm advisor, and that has been seen in the number of businesses that have gone independent over the years.

I have laid out several tips to help determine the right advisor for you who will lay out strategies tailored to your needs. This will be your trusted advisor and go-to person in helping you plan and build your retirement vault. But you may have noticed that I have not indicated what your advisor will be saying to you or advising you to do. Throughout this book, I have been discussing some specifics, and how you should be approaching them, but this is secondary to finding the right advisor. Once you have, then you will need to get down to business, as you work through defining and accomplishing your goals and mitigating your concerns. Next, I will go through some extra items that may help you tip the scale toward one advisor over another.

ADDITIONAL CONSIDERATIONS

When you meet with an advisor, it will be a mutual evaluation process: Do you want to work with him? Does he want to work with you? You should be open and honest about your financial goals, concerns, and objectives. The advisor will inquire about your current financial situation, and, hopefully, what your expectations are, both for him and your money. This is a critical process that allows you and your advisor to get on the same page. During this process you should get a feel for the advisor's personality and whether your objectives are in line.

To be well prepared and benefit the most from this first meeting, you should bring your financial information with you. Bring anything you want to discuss, and be prepared to answer basic questions about anything regarding your finances. This will let you focus on your goals and concerns and get the most out of the first meeting. Come prepared with objectives you want to discuss, but be open-minded; you may be exposed to something new in that first meeting that will help you, if you are willing to receive the advice.

You can also ask or find out about the advisor's community or outside activities. Most advisors treat their job like any other job. Others make it a mission to serve and help as many people as they can. This community involvement can be with the Chamber of Commerce, networking organizations, or service organizations. He may write a regular newsletter or articles in the newspaper. The advisor might even be on TV or the radio, spreading the word and trying to motivate people to take action and control of their finances. Very few of them will actually go to the trouble to write a book. All of these are indications of how proactive the advisor is in serving more and more people and continuing his business for years into the future.

If you have reservations about an advisor, but you like what you have heard from him, ask for references. If an advisor cannot give you the name (or several names) of happy clients, be concerned. He may even be able to give you the name of someone who has done exactly what he is proposing for you.

All of these are fairly subjective, and for good reason. There isn't a one-size-fits-all for choosing an advisor, and the right fit for you may be different from the right fit for someone else. Use this as a guide and follow your gut.

Bonus Chapter Eight
GENERATIONAL WEALTH

The biggest concern I see from wealthy investors is preserving their wealth. The volatility and uncertainty of the market in recent years has heightened this concern, and everyone remembers the huge market drops of 2008. Additionally, you want to limit your taxes, hedge inflation, and mitigate potential lawsuits from taking large bites out of your money. After all of that, you may not have thought too much about what will happen to your money after you pass away—whether you want it going to your kids, grandkids, church, charity, others, or some combination of these. All of these concerns must be addressed upfront to maximize your effectiveness. You also need to be confident that the money and assets you leave behind are used prosperously by whomever it is left to.

When you take the initiative to work with whoever will be taking over your estate on their intellectual wealth, then you can be confident that generational wealth will be there for your future generations. Generational wealth is the inherited money that is passed on when a person dies, if not before, for the generations to follow. Generational wealth is not only a dollar amount; more importantly, it needs to incorporate a mindset and a financial maturity that you pass on to your heirs. Without the intellectual wealth passing on to your heirs, any monetary wealth is just as likely to be squandered as preserved. For example, lottery winners go broke in no time at all because they do not know how to preserve the large amount of money that has been handed to them. Even with intellectual wealth, the money will not last multiple generations without a wealth-creating attitude. Having a wealth-creating attitude does not necessarily mean that the person needs to be an entrepreneur, although it helps. He or she does need to posses the same attitude toward wealth that the first-generation wealth creator had to create it in the first place.

Let's look at preserving the intellectual wealth. When we talk about intellectual wealth, we are really talking about responsible money management. If you already have adult children who will inherit your wealth, than you probably have some idea of their financial responsibility. Do they live within their means, balance their budget, and plan for the future? Do they seek professional advice when there are important matters at hand? If your kids are not responsible, or are too young for you to make that determination, then you will need to take steps to structure your wealth transfer so that the wealth will be used as you want it to be used. In many cases, clients feel that their wealth will be gone once the next generation takes control. This may be the case, and if that is what you are facing, then you have to choose how much to give them, and how much to put toward other purposes. One thing is certain—if you don't prepare and plan ahead, then the chance of your wealth becoming generational wealth is greatly decreased.

For the rest of you who have kids or heirs who are fiscally responsible, you need to work to enhance their intellectual wealth. You do this by building off their fiscal responsibility and getting them involved, or at least informed. If you haven't already told them about your assets, do so. It is important for their development and it will build a stronger bond between you. Explain how you earned, saved, or received it. Once they understand what's there, you can get them a little more involved. Do this by keeping them abreast of your financial decisions. Over time, you can get their opinions before you make your decisions. This process allows your heirs to grow and understand the wealth they will eventually control. More importantly, they will learn how to manage responsibly the wealth by watching you and working with you along the way. Over time, you and your heirs will maximize your intellectual wealth. When you talk to your heirs, make sure they understand what you expect from them; specifically, how you expect them to use and manage the assets once they are in control. Also make it clear what they need to do to take on more responsibility before you will hand over the keys to the castle.

You and your heirs should not hesitate to seek out professional advice for any areas of weakness. You can't know everything and it is reckless to act blindly, or without good information, when there are professionals out there to help your decision-making process.

You may be saying to yourself, "Well my kids are good people, but they don't posses all of these traits to the degree necessary to maintain our wealth for generations," and that is fine. The key to this process is to understand their capabilities. The next step is to seek out professionals and your critical employees to support this system when the heirs are weak or unwilling to participate. You may need professional advice in accounting, legal, and financial areas. Critical employees in a family business should also be elevated to the same level of importance as the professional advisors. They will become integral parts of the business's success or failure after the owner's death.

There are several things to keep in mind when picking your professional team. The first thing to look for in a professional advisor is someone you can trust, with a personality you can relate to and get along with. Remember, this professional team will also be working with your heirs, so they will need to interact well with each other, especially when you are not around anymore. To find a professional whom you can trust, get a referral from someone you know who has worked with a professional in that field. You can also ask other professionals you already work with to introduce you to a professional whom they know and trust. A leader in the industry, someone who has published something or is active with a professional organization or involved in the community, is another option. Whatever method you use to pick your professional, make sure he or she is someone you trust and can discuss things openly with.

The second criteria for selecting a professional should be competence within his field. This can be difficult for someone outside the professional's field to determine. However, you should be able to get some insight into their competence while the two of you are interviewing each other and discussing your circumstances. For example, let's assume you are seeking advice on transferring money to your kids or grandkids, still in elementary school. If the professional you are talking to is an attorney, then he should be able to give you specifics about the type of trust to use, and details about how it works. When you start asking questions about the investments inside the trust, I would expect the attorney to talk in generalities. Conversely, if you were talking to me or another financial professional, you should expect the discussion of trusts to be broad, but when we discuss the investments and risk/return aspects of the trust assets, etc., I will be specific and not beat around the bush.

The third consideration when selecting professionals is longevity. Do they have a successful business? Are they going to be in business in 10 years, or whenever you and your heirs need their advice? You may not see this as much of a concern, and figure that when this professional retires you can find another to do a comparable job—maybe you're right. But your heirs may not be as good at selecting the right professional if you are not around when the decision needs to be made. Working with a professional who has another 10–20 working years over another professional could be the difference that helps your generational wealth weather tough times. You can also select a professional who has teamed up with a younger professional, which would make their business transition seamlessly from one generation of clients to the next.

The fourth and final consideration when selecting the right professional is his understanding of your goals and concerns. Not only do they need to understand their specific task or professional involvement, but they also need to understand the personal dynamics that may affect things down the road. For example, your primary concern might be preserving capital, but your adult son would like to take more risk to potentially earn a higher return. Since it is your money, you decide the level of risk that will be taken, but there are ways to get your son involved without taking on risks you are not comfortable with. You may be okay with investing a small portion under your son's risk tolerance. Another option would be to discuss your concerns openly with your son: give him your perspective of risk, listen to his perspective, and then make your decision together. Even if you don't change your initial position, you now have him involved in the discussion. Also, if you have this discussion when you are meeting with your advisor, the advisor can answer questions you both may have, which may help you both reach a better understanding of each other's perspective.

When I meet with clients, the objective is to preserve their wealth through their lifetime, at the very least. If we cannot do that, then there is no point discussing generational wealth, since there may not be any wealth left to pass on. Once we have addressed the needs for the client's lifetime, we can start to determine what, if any, expectations the client has for his money after he is gone. Perhaps there's a charity that will receive some, or all, of the assets; otherwise, it is typically given to the client's children—and, left on their own, the kids might use the money, squander it, or grow it through their lives. Considering all of your options and being proactive can protect and teach the next generation how to handle money instead of it turning a "rags-to-riches" story into a "riches-to-rags" story.

If you want your wealth to endure for multiple generations, a wealth-creation attitude is critical. This is the attitude that got you where you are today. Most people fail to plan well enough to provide for themselves and their families. Even those who do typically spend down most of it during their lifetime, or at least expect to, and therefore do not see the value in any additional planning. But if you want your wealth to last for generations, you need to develop the wealth-creating attitude in your heirs. Again, this is not a one-size-fits-all process, but all generational wealth must have an underlying purpose. Without a purpose, the wealth will not last the test of time. Think about what drove you to accumulate wealth beyond what you intend to use in your lifetime.

Was it to provide a better life for your family and your family's family? Was it to support your church, community, or a charity? Maybe it was a combination of these things. Whatever it is, you have to have clarity of purpose. Write it down, discuss it, and get everyone on the same page.

Once the purpose is clear, you and everyone else can see how they can participate to promote the underlying purpose. If your heirs feel that this wealth is for them to use as they wish, then it's more than likely that they'll use it up during their lifetimes. For your generational wealth to be preserved, grow, and serve its purpose, your heirs have to support the wealth and not be a drag on the wealth. This takes as much effort as it did to create the wealth in the first place. But this doesn't mean that you have to groom your kids to be just like you. Frankly, it may be better if they aren't just like you. Having different personalities and skills work toward a common purpose can enhance the effectiveness of the decisions that are made. You want your heirs first to become independent professionally and financially, and then gain more responsibility and control over the generational wealth. There is an attitude and confidence that people develop when they are independent. You should guide and communicate with them, but you have to let them make their own decisions. Additionally, this will give you insight into how they will deal with money decisions going forward.

More important than financial independence is for your heirs to find their true calling in life. Finding your calling in life is more than doing something you are good at, although that is a critical part. You also have to find something you are passionate about. This is easier said than done, especially with today's tunnel-vision educational system. Most people either do something they are good at or something they enjoy doing, but not both. Over time, some people find a niche that allows them to do both. This is what I have found in my life as a financial strategist. I have the skills needed and the passion to maximize my effectiveness with my clients. This is what everyone wants to find. Someone with skills or schooling can do a good job at work, but if the passion isn't there, he will always be out-performed by those who do have the passion and drive to excel. He won't be as quick to improve or stay current in his field. He won't put in the extra work to make his products or services excellent.

Reaching the point where you are skilled and passionate about what you do makes all the difference. It opens up possibilities and income potential. Now you have reached the wealth-creating attitude. You have the skills and passion to be the best in your field. This is what you want for your heirs and anyone associated with your generational wealth. You want as many wealth-creating attitudes around your generational wealth as possible. Seek the best professionals to work with you. But more importantly, how do you encourage this trait in your heirs? They have to find their own way, so you can't show them the way. You can guide them, encourage them to continue to gain skills, and support them as they follow their passions in life.

In summary, to have your wealth become generational, you need three ingredients. First, your wealth must outlast you. Second, you need intellectual wealth, which includes the fiscal responsibility to manage money. Third, you want to attract and develop a wealth-creating attitude. This requires a common purpose and the internal drive by those involved to seek out work that they are passionate about. Once you see where your generational wealth stands, you can work to strengthen the weak links. You should also seek advice from professionals in areas of their expertise, especially areas where you and your heirs do not have experience or confidence. If your wealth is in a family business, all of these principles still apply; the interactions just get a little more complicated. I would not limit your generational-wealth heirs only to family members. Do not be afraid to incorporate those around you who not only support your generational wealth goals, but who can also effectively realize them. You should definitely consider incorporating new family members as they marry into the family, at least the ones you trust and believe will help the process. Or you may incorporate nonfamily members as professional support services, or as critical employees in your family business. You may feel comfortable enough with a nonfamily member to let them take a leading role in growing and preserving your generational wealth. However you choose to handle your generational wealth, do it proactively and keep the endgame in mind.

Summary

Throughout this book, I have tried to keep a constant theme. A theme of realistic expectations for your retirement and hopefully some clarity on what to look for as you create your retirement vault. I have covered a variety of investments, tools, and strategies that can help you plan your retirement proactively, instead of reactively.

My intention with this book is to show you my conservative approach to retirement planning. I firmly believe that predictability is essential. Many of my clients come to me without a good grasp on what their investments can realistically do for them in retirement. I make it my focus with my clients to provide specific expectations regarding what their money will do for them going forward.

In this book, I broke down in specific chapters each aspect of retirement planning. Breaking the retirement planning process down in this way allows us to look at each part independently. I focus throughout the book on predictability and limit the discussion of high-risk investments. The discussion of high-risk and high-return investments undermined the goals of many retirees to avoid losses, provide predictable returns, and, most importantly, to maximize retirement income.

I hope you have found the concepts and principles I have addressed throughout this book valuable and informative. Take action NOW and create your retirement vault.

Budget Breakdown

Category:	Item:	Item Total:	Sub Total:			
Home	Mortgage (Principle & Interest Only)		/mn			
	Property Taxes		/mn			
	Homeowners Insurance		/mn			
	Home Maintenance		/mn			
	Homeowners Association		/mn			
		Sub-Total:		/mn		/yr
Income Taxes	Federal Income Tax		/mn			
	Social Security (FICA)		/mn			
	State Income Tax		/mn			
	Local Income Tax		/mn			
	Medicare		/mn			
		Sub-Total:		/mn		/yr
Utilities	Electricity		/mn			
	Cable/TV		/mn			
	Water/Sewage/Garbage		/mn			
	Gas		/mn			
	Phone		/mn			
	Internet		/mn			
		Sub-Total:		/mn		/yr
Auto	Auto Payments		/mn			
	Auto Insurance		/mn			
	Car Repairs/Maintenance		/mn			
	Other Transportation (toll, bus, rental)		/mn			
	Car Tags & Registration		/mn			
	Fuel		/mn			
		Sub-Total:		/mn		/yr
Life & Health	Medical Insurance		/mn			
	Prescriptions		/mn			
	Dental Insurance		/mn			
	Vision Insurance		/mn			
	Disability Insurance		/mn			
	Life Insurance		/mn			
	Umbrella Policy Insurance		/mn			
		Sub-Total:		/mn		/yr

Gifts	Donations		/mn			
	Gifts (Birthdays, Anniversaries, etc)		/mn			
	Christmas Savings		/mn			
	Church		/mn			
		Sub-Total:		/mn		/yr
Food	Groceries		/mn			
	Dining Out		/mn			
		Sub-Total:		/mn		/yr
Entertainment	Vacation		/mn			
	Recreation		/mn			
	Hobbies (Golf, Fishing, etc)		/mn			
	Other		/mn			
		Sub-Total:		/mn		/yr
Misc	Education		/mn			
	Childcare		/mn			
	Clothing		/mn			
	Personal Care		/mn			
	Subscriptions		/mn			
		Sub-Total:		/mn		/yr
Debts	Credit Cards		/mn			
	Student Loans		/mn			
		Sub-Total:		/mn		/yr
Savings/ Investments	Savings		/mn			
	Retirement (401k, IRA, etc)		/mn			
		Sub-Total:		/mn		/yr

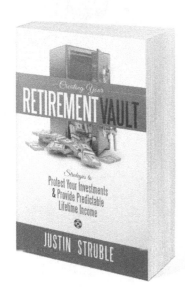

How can you use this book?

MOTIVATE

EDUCATE

THANK

INSPIRE

PROMOTE

CONNECT

Why have a custom version of *Creating Your Retirement Vault?*

- Build personal bonds with customers, prospects, employees, donors, and key constituencies
- Develop a long-lasting reminder of your event, milestone, or celebration
- Provide a keepsake that inspires change in behavior and change in lives
- Deliver the ultimate "thank you" gift that remains on coffee tables and bookshelves
- Generate the "wow" factor

Books are thoughtful gifts that provide a genuine sentiment that other promotional items cannot express. They promote employee discussions and interaction, reinforce an event's meaning or location, and they make a lasting impression. Use your book to say "Thank You" and show people that you care.

Printed in the USA
CPSIA information can be obtained
at www.ICGtesting.com
JSHW012056140824
68134JS00035B/3470